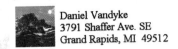

Daniel Vandyke
3791 Shaffer Ave. SE
Grand Rapids, MI 49512

For my mom :
The very first designer in my life,
and a continual inspiration.
Enjoy your new projects!

Much love,

Nicole

house beautiful

bathrooms

The Editors of House Beautiful Magazine

Louis Oliver Gropp

Editor in Chief

Margaret Kennedy

Editor

Text by
Sally Clark

hearst books ◆ new york

Library of Congress Cataloging-in-Publication Data
is available upon request.

ISBN 0-688-16750-0

PRINTED IN ENGLAND

First Edition

10 9 8 7 6 5 4 3 2 1

This book is set in Bembo.

www.williammorrow.com
www.housebeautiful.com

Editor: Alanna Stang
Designer: Susi Oberhelman

Produced by Smallwood & Stewart, Inc., New York

conte

The book before you will establish definitively that the bathroom, as it has evolved over the past several decades, is certainly one of this century's more gratifying and personally satisfying developments. Who among us doesn't treasure the pleasure of stepping into our tub or shower for the peace and quiet and renewal of this daily ritual. And what a place those showers and tubs, and their encompassing environments, have become.

We've moved a long way beyond the original five-by-seven-foot bathroom with tub, toilet, and sink lined up like soldiers in a row. Today a bathroom can be open to, and perhaps part of, the bedroom. It often expands beyond meeting simple hygienic requirements into exercise space, dressing room, even out into the garden. And the equipment itself—the fixtures and fittings, the steam and whirlpool equipment, the accoutrements for makeup and personal grooming, the variety of materials for tactile and visual pleasures—all add to the endless

possibilities. Not all of them have to be grand, although what could be more grand than a simple enclosure for taking a shower outdoors under the sun and the sky, one of the many possibilities included in the pages to come.

Discovered by HOUSE BEAUTIFUL's editors as they follow developments in architecture, design, and decoration for the monthly issues of the magazine, the bathrooms shown here come from all over the globe. We hope you'll find them inspiring, as you admire the handsome photographs, read the helpful text written by Sally Clark, and study the inspiring work by some of the best designers in the world.

Louis Oliver Gropp
Editor-in-Chief

... GOD SEES YOU, BUT HE UNDERSTANDS

What constitutes luxury in the bath? Obviously swank materials to start: stretches of silvery mirror, richly veined marble on walls and counters, gleaming touches of brass, chrome, or satiny nickel. A generous vanity surface, a large pedestal sink with roomy edges, a commodious tub to loll in—all are elements that lend a sumptuous feel. But space itself is perhaps the greatest luxury of all. The ideal room—at least for a master bath—is large enough to embrace a whirlpool soaking tub, a roomy shower niche, separate areas for a vanity or two, enclosed w.c.,

and perhaps an exercise area as well. The best sybaritic baths combine beauty with utility, and form with function. Multiple shower heads, electric towel warmers, and bath faucets that gurgle at the command of preset timers—these are just some of the mechanical amenities that make a bathroom a great pleasure. And what could be more indulgent than the bath that puts the user close to nature—a window filled with light, looking out on leafy greenery or summer-blooming roses, a bather seeking refreshment through a few moments of tranquility in her private refuge.

Translucent bricks filter shimmering light in a bath created by Brian Killian, a designer who loves to coax industrial materials into luxurious attitudes. Echoing the curve of the wall is a freestanding vanity ornamented with ceramic squares and triangles from Pewabic Pottery, a tile studio famous for its slightly iridescent earth-tone glazes.

A fine example of sky's-the-limit spatial indulgence is a contemporary open-plan master bath created by Santa Monica designer Brian Murphy, opposite. In masterminding the transformation of a 1950s house in the Hollywood hills, Murphy reconstituted a trio of boxy bedrooms and baths into a lavishly roomy master bedroom and bath complex.

A muscular, custom double vanity backs up against a frosted glass partial wall, right, that separates the spa from the sleeping area. Within the space, specific areas including closets and privy are sheltered in small chambers of aqua-tinted frosted glass. In a corner, a metal "towel case" holds stacks of white towels.

Sun-washed light plays across the gold and vanilla surfaces of a master bath designed by Paul Egee. The harlequin-motif floor of terra-cotta tiles feels pleasantly rough on bare feet. A vintage metal cabinet on tapered legs houses toiletries behind panels of clear glass. A pair of French doors, lightly covered with sheer fabric, lead outdoors.

crème brûlée

ith its profusion of custard tones, this bath is as sweet and soothing as a vanilla-laced dessert. But it's definitely not sugary. The room delivers a spicy punch with a series of harlequin-patterned elements: angled floor tiles colored in all-spice tones of brown and taupe, little diamond-print shades jauntily capping the sconces, diaphanous window scrims ending in handkerchief points. Paul Egee of Waterworks, in Danbury, Connecticut, conceived the bath in pampering terms, providing a generous volume of space in which vanity, tub, and shower are each accorded their own roomy quarters. No mere stall, the shower is a small room entered through a transparent sheath of tempered glass. Features are luxe: Twin brushed-nickel oval sinks arc handwrought, the bath displays a European hand shower, light streams through French doors that open to the garden. These elegant surroundings are meant for long-term enjoyment, not to be altered anytime soon. So Egee reached for a neutral color chart to provide the room with a gentle, easy-to-live-with palette. But beige does not equal bland. The designer tweaked the neutrals, mixing different tiles for walls and floors to achieve a subtly variegated spectrum that moves from vanilla to cinnamon. Rather than finish the walls with plain molding tile, he selected a decorative edging: From that wave-and-dot border came the harlequin motifs that wink laughingly from unexpected corners.

The zigzag decoration on the vanity might have been borrowed from Pierrot's famous clown collar. Featuring gumball-size gold spheres at the end of each point, the design is a witty detail that breathes oxygen into the dreamy beige bath. The custom-built vanity has other attractions: hand-formed washbowls glimmering with a brushed nickel finish, above, handsome European-style faucet sets, a capacious lower shelf to serve up extra face cloths and bath sheets. Above the vanity, two medicine cabinets fashioned after vintage models end in a small built-in bar that keeps soft linen finger towels in place.

Resting in the curved hollow of a bay window, the claw-foot tub surveys the bucolic panorama of a country garden, left. This is a spot for a bather to bask in the sun, entertain a daydream, page through a book. Setting a theme, playful harlequin shades top the nickel sconce lights, above right. Similar saw-tooth edges sparked by gold baubles turn up in the sheer window scarves, center right. A new version of an old design, the tub displays a painted-on decoration, below right, inspired by the two, slightly different, wavy tile motifs that appear just under the window and as an edging finishing off the wall tile. ◈

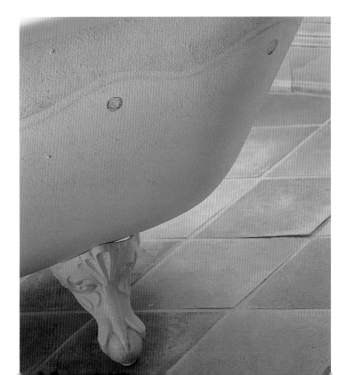

spaciousness   In a Long Island beach house inspired by the shingled cottages of the 1880s, New York designer Carl D'Aquino infused rooms with handcrafted details to convey a period atmosphere. In the master bath, above, tucked under the eaves of the gabled second story, the custom woodwork evokes the spirit of Victorian-era carpentry.

Another historic model, the Regency-era print room, prompted the Wedgwood-green master bath at designer Michael Stanley's Connecticut home, opposite. Conceived with the spacious dimensions of a library, it features a fireplace, a French fainting couch, and neoclassical art.

warmth

Modern never meant cold
as far as designer Benjamin
Baldwin was concerned.
Light and warmth suffuse
his pure and simple spaces.
For a house in Sarasota,
Florida, Baldwin created a
free-flowing master bath
that opens into a dressing
area. He provided the bath-
cum-dressing room with
ample storage by installing
streamlined built-ins—a five-
drawer chest in the dressing
area and an array of cabinets and drawers beneath
the vanity to hold toiletries
and towels. Baldwin always
worked with a limited
palette; for this bath he
selected marble veined in
his favorite cream-taupe-
beige color range and
applied it lavishly to floors,
walls, tub surround, and
vanity counter. Sparkling
mirrored niches for the tub
and vanity hold and reflect
the sunlight, making the
bathroom seem invitingly
large and open.

light   Cool colors and pale-toned materials automatically increase the sense of space. In his own Washington, D.C., cottage, designer Tom Pheasant used light oak cabinets and alabaster-toned laminate to create an airy haven, above. Defying the tight quarters, he sculpted a counter against one wall and set near it a curved vanity to cradle a round sink. Mirrors above the counter create the illusion of infinite space.

Pale ash cabinetry was designer Bruce Bierman's choice for the bathroom in his Manhattan loft, opposite. Raised one step from the vanity area—which also functions as a dressing room—the w.c. and low tub are screened by sliding ash doors fitted with light-filtering frosted glass.

indulgence

Luxe appointments borrowed from the past create stylish, cosseting spaces. San Francisco designer Gerald Jacobs translated his experience of stays at Europe's grand hotels ("I have fond memories of white mosaic tile and wonderful enormous tubs") into a pampering room with a deep turn-of-the-century soaking tub, left. Other details worth a five-star rating: a generous serpentine marble washbowl surround, original vanity legs revived with gleaming nickel, and a mirror-upon-mirror wall collage.

Evoking chic black-and-white baths of the 1930s, a shimmering room features walls in ivory marble shot with zebra-stripe veining of ebony, above. The black marble counters poised on shiny legs of tubular brass are another thirties-style element in the room designed by Stephen Byrns for an Arts and Crafts house on the edge of Lake Michigan.

Custom splendor: Displaying glimmering curls of stainless steel, the unique vanity in the master bath, opposite, has a French limestone base, mahogany drawers, and a view of the Pacific Ocean.

The powder room washbowl, above, is crafted of white bronze. The towel bar was fabricated to mimic the downward curve of the brushed chrome faucet.

lmost everything in the ultramodern bathrooms of this southern California house, including the sparkling stainless steel double vanity and the limestone-faced wading-pool tub, is a custom design. "We did buy the faucets, and the toilets are standard," says Catherine Herbst, the project architect who supervised the installation. The master bath and the powder room were designed by the San Diego architectural firm headed by Rob Wellington Quigley as part of a contemporary concrete, steel, and glass house that fronts the Pacific Ocean. The adventurous clients who commissioned the house, a couple with grown children, worked closely with the designers to develop the unique baths. The stainless steel vanity in the master bathroom, for example, began with a photograph of a bathroom in a hotel in which the owner once stayed. The grotto-like pool was also carefully customized. "We field-adjusted a lot of things, including the steps, to what was a comfortable height."

Site-built amenities such as the lantern-shaped shower room, left, and deep bathing pool, opposite, make these baths the ultimate in custom splendor. "The shower is the husband's space," says architect Catherine Herbst, the project architect for the Rob Wellington Quigley–designed project. "From the exterior of the house the shower reads like a beacon, and he loved the idea of bathing in a lantern." Faced with African multicolored slate, the shower's walls are paved in small white Japanese-crafted porcelain ceramic tiles that have rounded edges. The shower window is partially sandblasted for privacy, but clear on the upper section to provide a view of the coastal scenery. ◆

Mirroring in a bathroom is a glamorous touch. But it also serves the very practical role of reflecting light and lending an enclosed or windowless room the illusion of expansiveness. Here, an L-shaped vanity area that opens into a shower room and sequestered w.c. is really a windowless cul-de-sac inserted into the central core of a San Francisco apartment reshaped by Eric Haesloop, a principal in the firm of Turnbull Griffin & Haesloop Architects. Loathing clutter, the clients wanted storage systems to keep everything out of sight. Haesloop's design team obliged, devising storage concealed behind the continuum of mirrored doors that pull open with simple flat metal handles. Reflecting light from overhead fixtures, the bathroom's mirror-sheathed surfaces create the illusion of uninterrupted floating space. The absence of a window is never apparent.

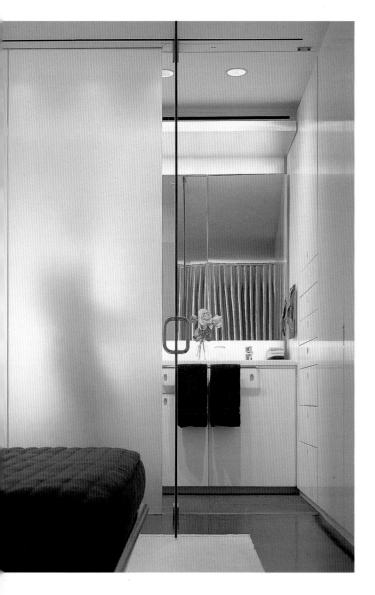

shimmer Membranes of glass can define space, usher in light, and lend crystalline modernity to a bath. The opaque-glass wall that architect Robert D. Kleinschmidt installed in his windowless master bath, above left, brings in natural light from the adjoining bedroom. In another bath-room that opens into a master bedroom—this time in a 1927 Paris apartment, above right—sliding panels of transparent glass were chosen by designer Paul Mathieu and his partner, Michael Ray, to suggest the jazz-age luxury of an ocean liner.

A sweep of subtly curved glass rising twelve feet forms a pellucid curtain for a double shower created by New York designer Beata Galdi, opposite. As a counterpoint to the slick stretch of glass, the floor is paved in charcoal slate with a matte finish. The sliver of a bath, remodeled from three small rooms, is a paragon of functional luxury.

fantasy

Picture escaping to a private lagoon. Against the seam-less blueness of the sky meeting the sea, there is a sheltering cove with a natural rock-carved pool of warm, eddying water. That restful fantasy inspired the serene personal spa created for the Kohler Co. by Billie Tsien and Tod Williams, who worked with project designer Matthew Baird. The whirlpool is set in limestone slabs, oppo-site, which extend into a surround, suggesting weathered rock circling a small blue bay of water. A miniature moss garden thrives on the blue-gray stone. Sandblasted glass panels define the shower area. To underscore the spa-like nature of the room, they installed a regulation gymnasium punching bag. Small turquoise and violet-blue sanded square glass tiles serve as wall paving.

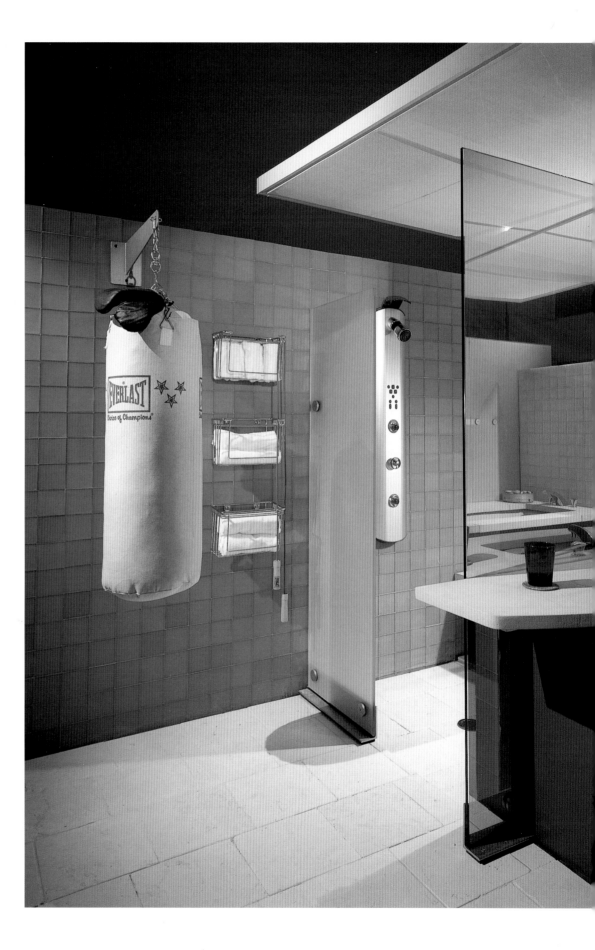

healthy luxury

"I wanted the armchairs to be very cozy," says Mark Bombara, who had the loungers made slightly over-scale to give them an embracing feeling. They're equipped with nickel casters so they can be pushed out of the way when floor space is needed for exercise. To encourage the feet-up rest that health experts advocate, the designer added a cushy ottoman.

People want to come home and feel like they are in their own private Canyon Ranch," says Mark Bombara, who masterminded a personal retreat devoted to the fine arts of exercise and massage. He describes it as "a room you can fall into to break away from the crazy pressures of the day." Plain cotton fabrics and an all-ivory scheme evoke the basic trappings of the no-nonsense health club. But the hygienic washable materials in which Bombara dressed the room belie its many hidden luxuries, including a couple of custom-built Bridgewater loungers, an oversize ottoman, and a splendid massage table crafted by the designer's expert upholsterer, Kevin McLaughlin. The chairs are exceptionally plush, made with pampering down-blend stuffing and down-wrapped backs. "I altered them for maximum comfort: They're a hair higher, and the arms cradle your arm," explains Bombara. To soften the space and absorb sound, he had yards of cotton duck stitched into a wall curtain.

Lures for the exercise maven include a rack laden with barbells, a stationary bicycle, and a state-of-the-art sound system. A large cheval mirror angled in a corner, just in front of the exercise bike, along with a trio of beveled mirrors on the opposite wall, has an expanding mission, reflecting light and extending the room. "They open up the space as if they were windows," explains the designer. The most luxurious fixture in this private health club is the custom-built massage table. The upholsterer who crafted it also produced the made-to-measure cotton terry cloth cover that fits snugly over the top, the tailored cotton twill skirt that attaches with Velcro strips, and the armchair covers that fasten up the chair backs by means of large fabric-covered buttons. Pull them off, toss them in the washer, and they are ready for another exercise session, just like a favorite sweatshirt. ◆

spas

The next best thing to lazing in an outdoor soaking tub is having a bathroom that opens into a garden. With French doors leading to a private deck, this sophisticated country bathroom in California offers the sublime experience of bathing and grooming surrounded by fresh air and greenery. Architect Howard Backen of Backen Gillam Architects in St. Helena, California, paneled the high-vaulted room, lofty as a small barn, in whitewashed Douglas fir and specified the same fir for the construction of the robust vanity. Mirrors set above the vanity give back abundant daylight and views from two pairs of French doors. Nestled into a surround of the same Douglas fir, the whirlpool nudges up against a large window framing a beautiful vista in every season.

Personal spas in vacation and weekend houses often take their design cues from the surrounding climate or culture. Following the rules of design for the traditional Islamic steam bath—or *hammam*—Elie Mouyal, a Paris-trained Moroccan architect, created a vaulted space dedicated to private ablutions, above left, for his own farm retreat outside Marrakech. Water gushing from a spout high on the wall pours into a limpid pool in the circular tub; an elegant cylindrical washbasin echoes the tub's shape.

While dunking in the large octagonal whirlpool under the eaves of a rambling Tudor-style weekend cottage on Long Island, above right, it is possible to enjoy beachfront views. Bath sheets embroidered with motifs of full-rigged vessels are a whimsical touch for a household of sailors.

In a Florida getaway, opposite, Washington, D.C., architect Hugh Newell Jacobsen created a master bath overlooking a grapefruit grove. The tub, beckoning like a pale blue private pond, is an aquamarine oval set into a gently rippled floor of precast concrete. The floor-to-ceiling window, with shutters for privacy, and the tall door exaggerate the height of the space.

In no other room do style and function come together quite so essentially as in the bathroom. A well-designed bathroom has to please the eye, but it also must work efficiently. Lighting needs to be plentiful and flattering, fixtures should feel substantial and operate easily, and surfaces should stand up to water and moisture, yet be pleasant to touch and brush up against. Every aspect of the bath, from the major components of tub and sink to such details as towel bars and faucets, should

be considered for performance as well as design.

Final choices must be influenced ultimately by personal taste. That may mean setting a vanity counter higher than the standard 36 inches to eliminate the discomfort of stooping over—a consideration even for those who are not particularly tall—or installing a combination of custom lighting units. Or it may mean doing extra research to find just the right design of wall-mounted toilet (important to the person who likes a clear floor under the w.c.) or the best-fitting corner bath tub (an excellent space-stretcher in small baths).

With its graceful curving form, the venerable rolled-rim claw-foot tub represents a fine union of beauty and utility. In a bathroom at the French country house of Pierre Bergé, a regal example holds center stage; a handheld shower attachment and soap caddy are the only embellishments to the classic tub.

The sunken tub may look glamorous and the gooseneck faucet may seem the last word in stream-lined fittings, but if painful contortionist maneuvers are necessary to climb in and out of the tub and the overarching faucet geysers water each time the tap is turned on full force, utility is ill served. In the best-designed bathrooms, performance works with style to create an environment that is as functional as it is alluring. Ultimately, design and utility must work in concert to create a bath that beguiles the eye and soothes the body.

Bathed in light streaming in through newly installed arched windows, an expansive aerie was carved from unused attic space. In front of the windows, designer Edgar Watkins built up the floor to afford the claw-foot tub picturesque views of the local Connecticut woodland. The damask-draped table centers the room and becomes a luxurious washstand, displaying Victorian antique hair brushes, combs, and toiletry bottles. The creamy damask, pebble-smooth porcelain fixtures including a pair of thirties-style pedestal sinks, above, and silvered oak floors form a trio of white tones, making the attic refuge decidedly spirit-lifting.

W H I T E

Drawing inspiration from
1920s architecture,
designer Ellen Roché
remodeled one bathroom,
opposite, in monochro-
matic white, installing
white ceramic tile-discs
on floors, blocks on
walls, and a shapely
porcelain sink-on-legs.

With a grand mirror
reflecting the palette
of clouds, designer
Jeffrey Bilhuber slipped
a cottage-style vanity
in place near a painted
dressing table, above.

All-white bathrooms are classic. In the all-white bath, texture is the subtle key to the room's beauty. Recalled from their former obscurity, splendid white vintage fixtures have been awarded a well-deserved revival. These graceful pedestal sinks, deep tubs, and curvy toilets bring a timeless quality to the functional aspects of the bath. Tile—on walls, floors, even ceilings—provides subtle texture; combining several kinds—perhaps cream squares with creamy relief borders or plain milk blocks with chalk-white rope edging—enriches the effect. Light fixtures should be suitably pale and minimal. Limiting accessories to white, silver, and glass assures the room a timeless elegance; fittings of chrome and nickel bestow a silvery sparkle; towels, of course, should be white, and luxuriously thick.

White, especially in bathrooms, can seem utterly timeless. A case in point is an all-white bath tucked under dormer eaves in a summer guest house. The Edwardian-style fixtures—a deep soaking tub and sculptural sink poised on a ribbed column—boast gleaming brass fittings, meticulously crafted as fine jewelry. A linen-draped stand steps in to serve as a vanity table and show off a lineup of sterling-topped crystal toiletry bottles. A peely-paint old porch chair and a vintage clock are other relics that seem to belie the advance of time. Above the tub, a map pinned to the wall encourages bathtime travel fantasies.

FIXTURES

Even for custom fixtures, the monolithic chunky sink and step-in shower at a California ranch house are exceptional. Like the walls of the house, custom-built by the owners, the bath furnishings are fabricated of "rammed earth," a syrupy mix of earth, sand, and cement that hardens into surfaces of stonelike texture and beauty.

The bathroom's major components—washbasin, tub, shower, and toilet—fall into roughly three groupings. In the first are commercial models available in a huge range of shapes and sizes. Designer fixtures are another choice; usually sold through specialist showrooms, they include imported European fixtures and artisan-made pieces, such as hand-formed copper washbasins or hand-painted vanity bowls. Custom furnishings comprise the third group, including showers built on-site and whirlpools and basins set off by one-of-a-kind deck and vanity surrounds. Custom furnishings do make for dazzling rooms, but are often mixed with readily available commercial fixtures for stunning results. Sometimes it's the fixture with the most unobtrusive silhouette that makes the greater statement.

In a small space, furnishings are all the more noticeable. The tiny room designed by Jeffrey Bilhuber is animated by a hand-formed metal basin that sits fontlike on a lilliputian vanity, above left. The unusual ceramic gold-rimmed circle that designer Celeste Cooper chose for a rinsing bowl displays the subtle texture of artisan-crafted claywork, below left. A sparkling disk of chrome just fits the postage-stamp-size counter of a bath by Joseph Lembo and Laura Bohn, opposite. A faucet operated by a foot pedal eliminates water taps, which in this installation would take up precious space.

pedestals

The pedestal sink is a fixture of unequaled elegance. Used widely in bathrooms from the Victorian era through the 1930s, its design is supremely versatile: The basin may be round or square, the column tapered or bulbous, and the overall scale grand or diminutive. A sleek modern version of the pedestal was the choice of David Salomon for his Southampton, New York, country house bathroom, opposite. But he bowed to tradition in color, selecting a classic white model as a contrast to the riotously colored patchwork of the tile walls, floor, and dado. The shapely silhouettes of the traditional pedestal sink may be American-style angular, above right, or the more European curvaceous cousin, below right. Both styles boast wonderfully wide rims that provide ample room for soaps, toiletries, folded hand towels, and even a hefty container of fresh flowers.

antiques

Vintage mahogany Gothic Revival chairs and a collector's horde of architectural prints would fool anyone into mistaking this room for a library. But the grand tub and the refined pedestal sink on a fluted column reveal the owner's real purpose in converting an extra bedroom with fireplace into a master bathroom. "The idea was to make it as comfortable as possible. It's a room in which to sit in the tub with the fire going," says designer Maria Emmett, who assisted designer Gaser Tabakoglu, the owner, with the magnificent transformation. A mahogany wardrobe discovered in London, an antique cross-legged table and shaving mirror, and curtains sewn from a real Paisley shawl all impart an old-world mellowness.

tubs

The white roll-edge tub, opposite, is a readily available commercial fixture. But the deck around it is designer Fu Tung Cheng's one-of-a-kind masterpiece, shaped exactly to the angled space. Handcrafted by the designer of poured concrete, the deck slab is embedded with tiny fossils and bits of coral and turquoise. Like a rock-enclosed mountain spring, the space is finished in natural stone, with slate walls and floor.

A completely custom tub can exceed the dimensions of mass-produced fixtures. The wavy-edged step-down soaking pool, right, designed by Jefferson B. Riley of Centerbrook Architects, is sunk into the sand-colored tile floor of a contemporary house in New York's Hudson Valley. Its expansive proportions allow for serious lounging and family fun.

A rolled-rim tub may be an old idea, but there is nothing passé about its graceful shape and comfort. In her London townhouse, designer Jane Churchill dressed a vintage tub with a surround of beaded board to match the room's woodwork, above left. A heated towel bar above the bath keeps linens organized and toasty warm.

After a day of riding at her Pennsylvania horse retreat, designer Mary Douglas Drysdale relishes a languorous soak in her remarkable deep copper tub, below left, a French antique she imported from Europe especially for the weekend house.

Positioned so that it looks out on a bower of leaves, the claw-foot tub in Michael Stanley's Connecticut country house, opposite, pampers even the tallest guests with its roomy, extra-long proportions.

A shower in its own dedicated space, whether a section of a bathroom or a completely separate room, is simple luxury. A bench to relax on while hot water sluices from an overhead nozzle is the only furniture needed in a shower room banked in beigey-pink limestone, designed by Gae Aulenti, left. A small casement window cut in the wall ushers golden light into the enclosure.

A circular shower ten feet in diameter, opposite, is a sybaritic feature the San Francisco firm of House + House designed for a master bath in a remodeled Tudor-style residence. Water rains from the large shower head centrally positioned overhead, but there is also an auxiliary hand shower that hooks to a wall fitting. Piped-in music and a purple-neon ring in the dome are other custom touches.

toilets

Although the basic shape of the w.c. has changed little since its refinement around 1900, the mechanism has improved with modernization. In a nod to environmental concerns, current models are built to utilize a lower water volume when flushed. The white porcelain toilet placed in an all-white setting, opposite, is the modern descendant of the unit first perfected by Englishman Thomas Crapper, who was awarded a patent for a valve-and-siphon design in 1891.

A more recent advancement is the Japanese-made toilet seat that provides bidet-like personal cleanliness. Seen in a room designed by Leslie Armstrong, above right, the washlet snaps into place and, when activated, releases a flow of warm water.

Another recent design trend is the custom-colored w.c. When designer Barbara Hauben-Ross transformed a powder room into a dazzling Miró-inspired masterpiece, she had the w.c. colored to match the hyacinth-blue background tiles, below right.

L I G H T I N G

A curvy sconce rests between the large mirrors attached to a pair of simply framed medicine cabinets by designer Barbara Barry, opposite. The mirrors capture and hold reflected daylight from a nearby window.

A sink alcove is a potentially dim space, but by angling a mirror in on three sides above a curved washbasin, above, the mirrored niche gives back light and reflects the miniature globe dangling overhead.

As a personal retreat, a room devoted to pampering and grooming, the bathroom warrants first-rate lighting. Unfortunately, all too many baths, even those in which no expense seems spared, fall short on that count. The ideal room has both general light to brighten the entire space and task light for specific areas such as the vanity. Windows and skylights strategically located to guard privacy guarantee a sweep of natural light by day. At night, and in dark rooms without much sun, well-placed fixtures provide a balanced bath of light. In a good lighting plan, individual areas of the room—the tub, shower, w.c., and vanity—are all well lit, augmenting general lighting. Specific lights are a must in large bath-rooms, especially those in which the tub or w.c. is in its own alcove. The absence of well-placed, specific light

can all too readily turn a tub or shower area into a dark and dreary cul-de-sac that is not appealing to spend time in. Adding dimmer controls to the switch is a good idea, as it assures a relaxing, softly lit ambiance while lounging in a tub or whirlpool and can be adjusted to allow reading as well. Grooming areas deserve special attention. The conventional installation—placing a fixture directly above the vanity mirror, either on the wall or ceiling—is not the best choice: Overhead fixtures often produce harsh downlight, casting distorting shadows on the face. A much better idea is to set a pair of light fixtures—whether sconces, tubes, or strips—on each side of the mirror, a placement that evenly washes the surroundings with a face-flattering glow of light. Finally, the selection of the light bulbs themselves should not be random. Lower wattage bulbs prevent the harsh shadows created by too-bright bulbs. Pink shading and warm tones, available even in fluorescent bulbs, are the most flattering to the figure and soothing to the soul. And for pure relaxation, candlelight remains unsurpassed.

In reinventing a master bath, California architect Victoria Casasco installed large light-giving windows and a glass door, then added a huge circular skylight to funnel in even more daylight. An ingenious custom vanity, designed as an island that will eventually be moved to a larger house the owners are planning, features back-to-back basins and mirrors. Casasco placed a pair of modern sconces on either side of a support column. At night when they are switched on, the glass-shaded sconces cast a shimmery glow.

An admirer of industrial
furnishings, designer Brian
Killian is adept at working
them into installations
with meticulous finish and
detailing. An example is the
large circular window he
created for a contemporary
bath, left. Its lower half
is a sandblasted shield
of privacy that still admits
light; the upper half is
transparent, allowing a
bather in the sunken tub a
clear view of the leafy
awning of branches outside.

A translucent window
works well as part of a plan
devised by architect Steve
Ehrlich, opposite. Flooded
with daylight, the space
also boasts specific lighting
for different sections of the
room, including overhead
spots in the shower area
and a strip of incandescents
above the vanity.

In a California house in
which most of the rooms
look out on plants, trees,
and garden courts, the
late architect Paul Rudolph
inserted a floor-to-ceiling
window in the master bathroom, opposite. The ocean
of general light the window
provides is supplemented
by twinkling incandescent
lights above the vanity and
a downlight over the sloping
custom-built, tile-paved tub.

Developed originally
for commercial installations,
glass blocks are an excellent choice for guarding
privacy and filtering light
in residential spaces. The
all-white marble bath at
fashion designer Geoffrey
Beene's Hawaiian vacation
home, right, is a snowy
white sanctuary, its privacy
preserved by a window of
glass blocks.

S U R F A C E S

In children's bathrooms tile-
covered surfaces are easiest
to maintain. Pulling primary
colors from a kid's paint box
and pairing them with black
and white, designers Barry
Goralnick and Michael
Buchanan coated walls, floor,
and counter with two-by-
two-inch ceramic tiles. By
arranging the small squares
in bold fields of color,
the designers brilliantly
disguised the room's
conventional proportions.

In a room where water splashes and puddles, where condensation and steam soak the air, and where toiletries and cosmetics often spill, surfaces have to be able to take a dousing. A range of water-shedding materials provides a wealth of choices. Dividing them into two groups—natural and synthetic—helps in surveying the options. Natural stone materials such as limestone, marble, and slate are handsome sheathings for floors, walls, counters, and fixture surrounds. Marble and granite, however, are hardly indestructible; they should be sealed, as they are liable to stain and scratch if they are not treated with great care. But ceramic tile, another classic natural material, is incredibly versatile. Available in a huge array of sizes, colors, shapes, styles, and finishes, it shrugs off water while providing high-style protection to surfaces. With the installation of tile, the combination of patterns and shapes, the grout width, and even the color of the grout contribute to the variety and stylishness of tilework design.

Synthetics—both solid-surface materials and decorative laminates—are popular choices for counters. When it is correctly fitted, decorative laminate is a water-impervious surface for shower and tub surrounds. Both the solids and laminates are made in a spectrum of colors and myriad designs, including fool-the-eye granite and marble, as well as a range of finishes from matte to glossy. Some new-age synthetics are more malleable than wood and can be cut, drilled, sliced, and sculpted into environments of truly waterproof modernity.

Waterproof wall treatments of tile, wainscotting, or mirror are most practical too. But bathrooms that are infrequently used, such as those at a weekend cottage, city pied-à-terre, or guest baths, can accommodate more delicate and dramatic coverings: rich wallpapers and luxe fabrics will survive occasional exposure to moisture.

Never afraid of pattern, designer David Salomon pulled out the stops in the tilework of a room he expanded and updated. With the tub nudged into a freestanding position, he dramatized it with a tile surround accented by black lozenges and licorice borders. Not quite finished, he rolled out a harlequin-patterned floor and moved a checkerboard up the walls of the shower. Plain walls would not do, of course, so he paraded a marching band of painted gray-stenciled diamonds across the untiled walls, right up to the ceiling.

Concrete is often viewed as a low-tech industrial material. In fact, the renowned architect Louis Kahn elevated unfinished concrete to elegant heights in buildings he designed fifty years ago. More recently, California designer Fu Tung Cheng has explored concrete's water-resistant properties for stylish residential bathrooms. The huge slablike counters he introduced into a tranquil bathroom, opposite, were custom-crafted from poured concrete. Slate pavers form a water-resistant backsplash.

Giant planes of concrete evoke monolithic modern sculptures in a Caribbean bath, above and below right, created by Antonio Morello and Donato Savoie of Studio Morsa. Walls, partitions, towel ledge, and washbasin surround are all fashioned of concrete. The floor, too, is cement, polished to a silky radiance with oily coconut fiber.

Beige and ivory honed limestone walls and floor cast a serene early-dawn glow in the master bathroom of a modern Southern California home designed by architect Barry Berkus and his daughter-in-law, interior designer Dana Berkus, opposite. Sunk into slabs of the same sealed stone, a low-rise whirlpool bumps up against the crystal clear shower. The tempered glass shower door forms a nicely transparent counterpoint to the solid walls.

Frosted glass and mirror gleam in a bath the color of creamy pearls, above left and right. To expand the room to infinity, San Francisco designer Paul Vincent Wiseman placed a large mirror in front of the vanity and set mirrored panels at the end of the bath alcove. For privacy, he specified frosted glass for the shower door and window. As a fine point in a room of impeccable details, Wiseman had matching borders sandblasted on the glass and mirror panels, giving the surface materials a unified, custom-tailored finish.

FLOORING

The dazzling trompe l'oeil "rug" that Vicente Wolf tossed on the floor of a bathroom, opposite and above, is a tour de force of decorative tilework. Set at a bold angle so that it stretches from the vanity into the shower, the rug displays a robustly scaled Greek key border. The whole motif has the powerful effect of pushing back the walls and visually enlarging the sliverlike space.

The ideal bathroom floor combines attractiveness with comfort and ease of maintenance. Ceramic tile encourages an array of patterns, colors, and design motifs, and wins out when it comes to durability and maintenance. Marble and slate offer the texture and color of stone; the mat surface of honed marble is the best choice for floors as polished marble tends to be slick. Wood is more comfortable on bare feet than stone or ceramic tile. Linoleum, cork, and rubber tile are some less obvious materials; cushiony to walk on, they come in an ocean of patterns and colors. Carpeting, of course, is soft and sumptuous looking. The best floor solution is likely a combination of materials: perhaps wood for the main area, ceramic tile near the shower and tub, and rugs for barefoot comfort near the bathing area and vanity.

Natural flooring materials lend character and subtle coloration to the overall design of a bathroom. Stone imbues a bath with distinctive good looks. A handsome slate floor, left, was chosen by Atlanta designer Nancy Braithwaite to set off a hearty vintage-style sink in a North Carolina mountain retreat.

Wood is prized by designers for the warmth it brings to a room, which is probably one reason designer Jed Johnson and architect Alan Wanzenberg chose tawny planks for the floor surrounding a sunken hot tub, opposite. With all wood floors, except those of water-impervious teak, care must be taken to immediately mop up puddles; standing water can eventually damage a wood floor's finish.

DIMENSION

In a contemporary house custom-built to take advantage of a riverfront setting, the Texas firm of Lake/Flato configured space into four stories, with the master bath enjoying its own sky-lit, double-height volume on the third floor, opposite. Dramatically smaller but no less striking is the tiny guest bath architect Evan LeDuc designed for a Michigan farmhouse, above, in which the basin fits snugly into an antique painted pine chest of drawers.

Until very recently, most full bathrooms were a conventional five-by-seven feet. (About half that size formed the customary powder room.) But modern life seems to require more fixtures, more appliances, more storage, and, thus, more space. Baths for children or weekend guests are commodious enough for a separate tub and shower, an extended vanity with two good-sized basins, and a closed-off toilet area. As for the master bathroom, it has exploded into a space that may harbor a complex of smaller rooms designed for exercise equipment, a spa with whirlpool, a walk-in shower, and sometimes a dressing area with space for a dressing table, wardrobe, and even a laundry room. Still, it is possible to squeeze the essentials into the most minute area without any sacrifice of style, provided every inch of space is considered.

In master bedrooms and guest rooms where privacy is not an issue, merging bedroom and bath creates an appealing open and airy space. Such connected quarters are part of the contemporary house in Santa Barbara designed by Arn Ginsburg.

A wall of folding panels opens to provide a view of the courtyard and sky above, while a window in the bathing alcove becomes a postcard of the garden beyond. Neutral grays, blacks, and whites join the shared bed and bath spaces together visually.

With deft placement and the right fixtures, attic spaces can be successfully converted into charming bath aeries for guest rooms and family bedrooms. Under sloping beams, architect Lester Wertheimer carved out space for a full-size bathroom, left. By running the vanity counter back to the window wall so that it becomes part of the tub surround, he tied the room together and expanded open storage space for toiletries.

In a Telluride, Colorado, country retreat, the pointed arch of a dormer window becomes a sheltering niche for a vanity, opposite. Beaded board on each side of the vanity provides an old-fashioned, splashproof surface, and its shiny white paint brilliantly reflects the flood of sun through the window.

Partitioning off the w.c. shelters the area and lends it the private feeling of a room within a room. The curtaining device may be an actual structural wall, partition, or decorative screen. In a New York City loft, left, architect Joan Dineen strategically placed a maple cabinet so that it sequesters the w.c. The glass shelves above it complete the partitioning effect while leaving the room open and airy.

In a Zen-like landscape complete with its own rock garden, Frederick Fisher placed the toilet behind an intriguing barricade of bamboo, opposite. The tapered stalks form a shadowy curtain that shields the fixture without intruding on the room's open feeling.

STORAGE

Imposing order on a large master bath by architect Ann Kalla, a capacious closet provides plenty of shelves for extra linens and tissue, opposite. Metal coat hooks inside the door act as a silent valet, presenting a fresh terry robe when the door swings open.

A grid of metal mesh baskets is an innovative way to store rolls of bath tissue in a bathroom, above.

The tiniest bathroom becomes much more appealing when there is some type of cabinet or cupboard to serve up extra hand soap, tissue, and finger towels. A multishelf floor-to-ceiling cupboard is an ideal solution for a family bathroom because it can house an array of towels, toiletries, and grooming items, organized by shelf for each member of the family. Cabinets and drawers that close guarantee some degree of neatness.

Family baths and master bathrooms designed for couples should have numerous towel racks, with some placed next to the tub, shower, and vanity and others positioned around the room. Open storage around the tub and vanity assures ready access to frequently used items; eschewing that utilitarian look, many designers pull in decorative trays, silver bowls, or baskets as hold-alls.

There is nothing like custom-built cabinets and drawers to organize storage and keep a bath forever tidy. Underscoring the spareness of a contemporary retreat with a glassed-in shower room, Manhattan designer Melvin Dwork specified an expanse of white cabinetry with metal pulls, left. The storage wall incorporates a large linen closet and an array of drawers for toiletries and grooming paraphernalia, guaranteeing the pared-down space an immaculate appearance.

To enliven the built-in cabinetry beneath a double-sink vanity, Boston designers Lee Bierly and Christopher Drake chose a handsome combination of palomino and ebony finishes, opposite. As a contrast to the clutter-free space, the designers created a ladder-like wooden fixture for towels beside the shower. Reaching up six rungs and encased in a frame-like wood molding, the unique towel holder is as handsome as it is useful.

A creative mix of open and closed units provides an ideal range of storage options. It's about "the play of shape," says Boston designer Celeste Cooper, who dabbled in geometry to wedge enough storage into a small space, opposite. Dreaming of trapezoids, she built a three-tiered towel tower above a make-up counter and angled drawers beneath. To keep the composition from skittering dizzyingly off balance, she imposed an orderly grid of white-grouted gray tile on the room.

Challenged by the confines of a regulation size bathroom, architect S. Russell Groves chose an airline-compact stainless vanity with handy towel slots and a triple-door medicine cabinet that conveniently absorbs the clutter, above left.

A custom vanity incorporating a concealing cabinet with a trio of open towel shelves was California designer April Sheldon's smartly conceived solution for revamping the bath of a 1950s ranch house, above right.

V A N I T I E S

A dressing table by Frank
Lloyd Wright, opposite,
is built into a snug corner.
The large wall-mounted
mirror reflects light from
a nearby window.

For a Long Island
beachhouse, designer
John Saladino placed an
antique metal dressing
table in the clean-lined
master bathroom, above.

From a 1930s Art Deco masterpiece to a very simple
custom-crafted laminate-sheathed model, the dressing
table is as useful as it is luxurious. A special place for an
intimate moment of reflection, or an efficient hub for
the day's ablutions, the vanity should be close to a window to take advantage of natural light for applying
cosmetics, and well lit at night by flattering illumination.
Mirrors should be in ample supply. The counter must be
large enough so that toiletries can be laid out, and several drawers should be available to conceal grooming
items. Room for a cushiony little slipper chair or pouf is
always a nice touch. Beautiful accessories—Venetian
glass jars, an ebony-and-brass hand mirror, vintage perfume bottles—provide a most personal feeling, and fresh
flowers are the final luxurious element.

London designer Nina Campbell selected an exquisite array of brushes, combs, and bottles for an ivory vanity table nestled in front of hand-kerchief-sheer curtains, opposite. The fine design of each accessory, from the curvaceous crystal base of the lamp to the wafer-thin mirror, contributes to the pleasure of the owner's morning toilette.

In a spacious master bath, above, designers Joseph Lembo and Laura Bohn devised a scaled-up counter to accommodate a central vanity area flanked by an oval sink at each end. Personal bibelots—photographs, a ticking time-piece—conspire with wall mirrors in unmatched old frames to lend patina to the newly crafted custom counter. For ballgown glam-our, the designers stitched a bath curtain of gray taffeta and hung it on spaghetti-strap ties.

ACCESSORIES

To exhibit small silver containers, Boston designer Elizabeth Speert chose glass shelves with a chrome gallery edge and interspersed opal and celadon glass perfume bottles among the silver, opposite. A medicine chest with a Venetian-style mirror complements the display.

Cream roses bobbing in a silver cup and an ivorine-handle brush are grace notes in a room by Manhattan designer Ned Marshall, above.

Details bring a bathroom to life. As with the decoration of any space, the accessories in a bath should be chosen to underscore the room's style. The traditional bath with mahogany cabinets and a claw-foot tub might display a tufted ottoman, a canterbury to hold magazines, or a collection of prints to enrich the walls. By contrast, the contemporary refuge may be a room so spare that its sole adornment is a sculpture reposing on the vanity.

A bath's functional details, including faucets, water taps, and towel bars are important accessories, too. Quality and craftsmanship count. The styling and ease of use of faucets and taps are noticed every time they are touched, and consideration should be made for young and old hands alike. The simplest design, of the best quality the budget allows, is always the wisest choice.

A sheet of mirror sliding across a window was designer Melvin Dwork's solution for a remodeled vanity niche backing onto a window wall, opposite. A track light above augments the streams of daylight pouring through the window.

As a companion to an oval nickel washbasin in a Florida bathroom, above right, Hal Martin Jacobs selected a sleek stainless-steel shaving mirror. The mirror flips to a magnifying surface on its reverse side.

Proving the advantage of a pair of small mirrors, designers Joseph Lembo and Laura Bohn affixed a retractable shaving mirror to the wall above a wash-bowl and placed a vanity mirror on the counter, below right. In the pared-down custard-colored space, the elaborate handcrafted silver frame of the looking glass has an exotic elegance.

By ushering into the bath furnishings more customarily encountered in a living room—a big club chair, artwork, an upholstered slipper chair—designers Joseph Lembo and Laura Bohn infused a master bath with the warm casualness of a private study. A recycled wooden flat from the garden straddles the salvaged tub as a toiletry tray. Another recycled gem is the tiny wood-and-steel side table by the tub: It once did service as a stool in a Singer sewing machine factory.

W

Close the door on the world. The bathroom is the one place in the house we can escape to and while away a few private minutes each day. Next to the bedroom, the bathroom is the room where we are most at ease and fully ourselves. A private refuge, it gains warmth and charm with decorative elements that have a personal stamp. If soft coral is a favorite color, think of the delicious pleasure of starting the day surrounded by walls glazed that sun-drenched shade. Preconceived notions of limiting bathroom furnishings to utilitarian objects have been

himsy

At the London-based design firm of Colefax & Fowler, Roger Banks-Pye's job was troubleshooting, so he was unfazed by the tiny bath in his own flat. Cut-out squares in blue-and-white checks chase the boredom of white walls. As a wry note he added an accessory the French refer to as a chaise-percée; it transforms the w.c. into a seat of thronelike decorum.

firmly abandoned. Mementos as humble as beach-gathered shells or as splendid as heirloom silver are unexpected details that lend surprise and humor. A woman who inherited beautiful sterling dining accoutrements, including a Buccellati lemon strainer, keeps them polished and displayed on built-in shelves in the bathroom, where she enjoys them every day. One man displays smartly framed turn-of-the-century baseball ephemera in his wood-paneled spa. Any injection of whimsy, whether priceless or penny-ante, further personalizes this most personal of rooms.

Contrary to the popular belief that prints overwhelm small spaces, pattern actually works well in tiny baths. The colorful all-over designs lift the room out of the ordinary and endow it with personality. Rather than extensively remodel the 1930s baths in his Manhattan apartment, Mark Hampton refreshed them with pattern. A garden of floral fabrics in his wife's bath, above left, blooms against trompe l'oeil wallpaper that gives the illusion of shirred fabric. To the ceiling and walls of his own bathroom, above right, he applied a Gothic Revival paper originally designed by Pugin in the nineteenth century for the Houses of Parliament.

Faux-grained mahogany woodwork and a Regency cabinet transformed the standard-size bath into a clubby refuge.

A floral printed fabric shirred on walls enlivens a bathroom by Mario Buatta, opposite. A trellis-motif carpet and dainty slipper chair in rose checks play off the signature chintz.

When cast-iron tubs were introduced in bathrooms, around 1880, they were an immediate success. Poised on claw feet, curved to the shape of the bather's back, these vessels of indulgence encouraged long and languorous soaks. They are still luxurious. Designer Han Feng moved a salvaged antique tub into her Manhattan loft, opposite. On warm days, with the door to the roof deck ajar, the deep rolled-rim treasure invites relaxation.

In a famous English country house where virtually every surface became a canvas, Vanessa Bell transformed the bath surround with her own idiosyncratic painted brocade of pattern and color, above right. Another salvage operation was masterminded by decorative artist Lyn Le Grice: She revived an antique footed tub in an old house in Cornwall, England, below right, by adorning the sides with wispy stenciled wreaths.

Walls of pumpkin-and-marigold stripes energize an otherwise sedate all-white bathroom. Designers Ronald Mayne and DeBare Saunders hung the striped paper horizontally, a tactic that seems to expand the space of the standard-size room. Quirky accessories, including a totemlike wood carving next to the pedestal sink and a comical image of a bathing beauty propped up on the tub, inject an idiosyncratic charm. A diminutive Victorian antique chair and a Gothic-style antique shaving mirror positioned at the end of the tub are unexpected notes of luxe in this lively scheme.

A bather is showered with light and able to take in tree-and-sky views in the glass-ceilinged shower room of an Oregon vacation getaway. Jeffrey Biben and Peggy Bosley, husband and wife architects from Claremont, California, designed the room for their family's wood-and-glass forest retreat overlooking the Willamette River. From the outside, corrugated metal sheathing the shower enclosure evokes vernacular cabin construction. Inside, the crescent-shaped shower room is part of a sophisticated yet spare open-plan bed and bath suite. The simple vanity offers such functional features as large twin washbowls and generous open and closed storage beneath its laminate-clad counter. The shower's white tile walls are pierced by two tiny casement windows that allow for summery breezes and covert bird watching.

Like a grand picture window, the curved glass and glass-brick wall of a demilune shower provides the exceptional experience of showering surrounded by nature. Richard Elmore, a Palo Alto, California, designer, created the space as a semicircular private enclave, then doubled its luxurious potential by installing two powerful showerheads and adding a pair of entrances from the bath area. The light-filled main room, conceived as a private spa, is dominated by a deep whirlpool tub; its surround and wide ledge are sumptuously finished in gray-veined Carrera marble, as are the floor and vanity in this truly sybaritic room. A door near the tub leads out to a lushly planted terrace.

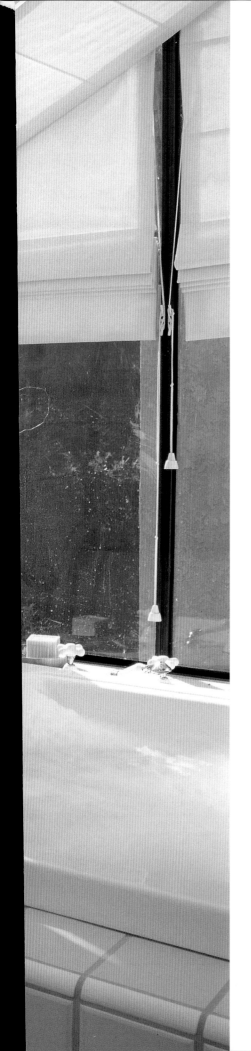

For a Hollywood screen-writer, architectural designer Van-Martin Rowe scripted the dramatic scenario of a solarium tub, opposite. Expertly fitted custom shades afford privacy and control light.

Envisioning a swank studio apartment for a gentleman architect, French designer Marie-Paule Pellé whimsically enclosed the bath in a half-finished framework, above right. While the fantasy setting, built for a Paris showhouse, may seem a bit far-fetched, the chic black-and-gold Empire-style tub lends itself wonderfully to an American master bath. Another French designer, Julie Prisca, introduced sleek modernity into the rustic bathroom of her 1820 Normandy retreat by adding stylish metal furnishings—chair, wash-stand, screen frame—of her own design, below right.

Washing off in an outdoor shower at the end of a lazy day on the beach is a delicious pleasure. On a Manhattan roof terrace, above left, floral designer Paul Bott built an outdoor shower, a tongue-in-cheek whimsy in a city where taller buildings look down on it. Its beaded board walls, flexible shaving mirror, and graceful side table for soap, sponges, and a loofah, above right, would be at home in any country house.

The outdoor shower attached to a Maine guest house designed by Mallory James Interiors, opposite, is an elegant affair, with a slatted floor for water run-off and fancy lattice-and-lace millwork. A metal towel bar on the wall just outside the swing-out door keeps fluffy bath sheets close at hand.

Architect Walter Chatham designed a sprawling private haven with every conceivable comfort. The showpiece is the generously proportioned whirlpool tub, with seating areas fore and aft. A private vanity with built-in counter, sconces, storage, and hair dryer is tucked into a closet.

last resort

y philosophy is that buildings should take you away," says Walter Chatham. "This bathroom, created with the Kohler Co., is a warm and sunny place, even when it's winter outside." Chatham is a New York City–based architect noted for the freshness of his contemporary thinking as well as his design work at such warm-weather communities as Seaside in Florida. Taking inspiration from the *plein air* cabanas that dot resort beaches all over the world, he created a pampering spa that brings home the excitement of a vacation getaway all year long. The room is filled with resort-worthy amenities including a jumbo whirlpool, a wood stove to toast the air on chilly days, two spacious seating areas with plush chairs and sofa, a roomy shower, and an enclosed w.c. and bidet. Packed into three huge closets are supplies, a media center, and a vanity. Chatham updated the classic American bathhouse by using modern materials: Corrugated steel barrel vaults underscore the room's lofty height, and an illuminated frosted-glass skylight washes the room in light, even on overcast and rainy days. The state-of-the-art plumbing technology includes a shower with hydromassage. But Chatham selected fixtures with a vintage look to stir memories of the baths once built at seashore resorts. The horizontal bars of color on the doors are another souvenir from idyllic beach outings: Squint, and they'll evoke canvas cabana awnings flapping in the wind on a July day.

By scooping out pockets of space along each side of the whirlpool, Chatham incorporated an array of amenities into the spa. Separate niches provide privacy for a pair of porcelain pedestal sinks. The architect sheathed the walls behind the sinks with mirrors topped with moldings to create the illusion that the looking glasses are windows to the world outside. Behind one floor-to-ceiling awning-striped door is a built-in media center. Another door conceals a generous supply of towels. The curvy sofa and lounge chairs opposite it are slipcovered in ocean-blue cotton toweling.

With its overhead spigot, hydromassage option, and adjustable body sprays, the enclosed stall offers the last word in shower convenience, opposite. As playful details, the architect piled sand-colored tiles up along the shower wall, let loose mosaic fish to cruise along the shower floor, and spilled azure tiles and an ocean-wave border under the w.c., right. The tropical yellows, oranges, and aquas of the tiles and the mosaic's rough surface give the shower a hand-crafted warmth that belies its technological modernity. ◆

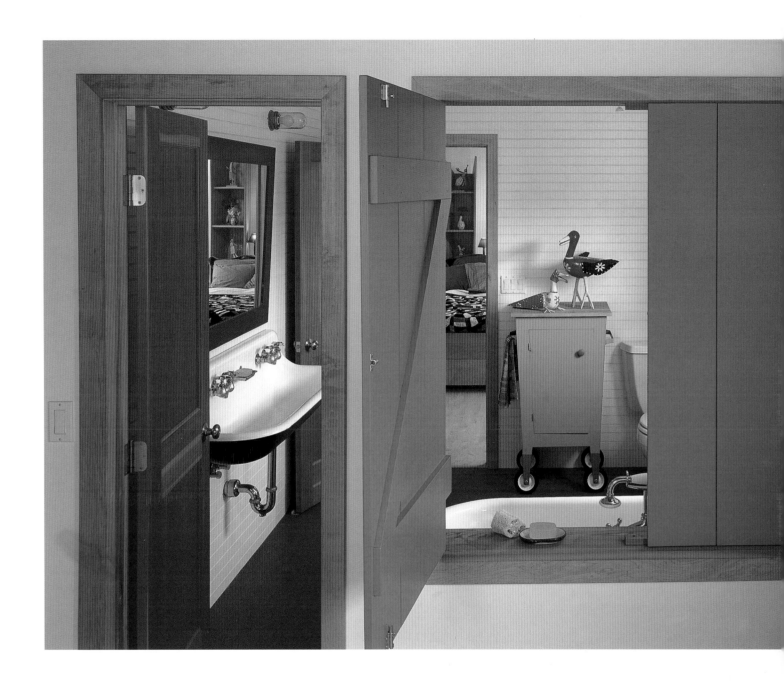

Heartland inspirations: His affection for Amish quilts prompted Van-Martin Rowe to create a colorful patchwork ceramic tile floor in a bathroom for two young children, opposite. A parade of riotously colored abstract tiles forms a border on the vanity.

For an artist's house built in an agricultural landscape in the Midwest, New Haven architect Turner Brooks devised a large bathroom with elements coyly borrowed from a milk house— a troughlike sink, enamel-painted beaded board, and barn-door interior shutters.

Intrigued by the Directoire style, Parisian designer Frédéric Méchiche re-created the atmosphere of late-eighteenth-century France throughout his Paris duplex—even in the bathroom. A refinished antique zinc tub reigns in the center of the room, majestically elevated on an old stone platform. Behind it, Méchiche hung a pair of *grisaille* landscapes, setting each one within a full-length niche framed by slender columns. Though the room is authentic right down to its cream and black antique stone floor, a modern heating system was installed beneath the tiles.

In one guest bath of a
Mediterranean getaway,
opposite, designer Mimmi
O'Connell capitalized
on local artisan crafts, laying
a terra-cotta floor, molding a
curvaceous stucco vanity,
and whitewashing every
surface, including the basket-
weave-paneled door. Then
she gave the room a chic
turn by hanging a pair
of darkly burnished sconces
and an elaborate mirror
with a black-and-gold painted
frame. In another guest
bath, above, the designer
produced a unique wash-
basin by setting a painted
Majorcan bowl into a
funnel-like pedestal of milk-
white stucco.

ondon-based designer Mimmi O'Connell is
known for rooms that have a slightly under-
done insouciance. Her work is the exact opposite
of those perfectly groomed but lifeless hotel-like
interiors that are mistakenly called "proper decorat-
ing." It is just such places O'Connell enjoys taking
down a few pegs, moving out the rigid British uphol-
stery and bringing in slouchy chairs slipcovered in
cotton ticking, one or two exceptional Continental
or Asian pieces of furniture, and a few oddball
ironwork accessories. Then she relaxes the whole
scheme with the patterns and colors of rugs and fabrics that she has gathered on buying forays to Hong
Kong, France, Thailand, and other ports of call. The
marvelous paradox of an O'Connell-designed space
is that it never looks as though a designer had set
foot in it. The all-white baths O'Connell devised in
a vacation retreat in Majorca, the island paradise off
the eastern coast of Spain, are fine examples of her
underplayed style. By combining the white stucco
and terra-cotta materials typical of a Mediterranean
farmhouse with a few carefully edited haute decor
furnishings, she created seductive bathrooms that are
havens of rustic opulence.

Into the white stucco
master bath O'Connell
introduced furnishings of
refined elegance—fine,
light-filtering Irish linen
curtains to dress the
window, a thick natural
jute tassel to lend a sumptuous detail to the iron
curtain rod, a vanity table
luxuriously draped in white
linen, and a dainty black
lacquered nineteenth-
century vanity mirror to top
it off. A delicate black-
painted chair is a dramatic
contrast against the
room's snowy whiteness.

Pristine white walls, sloping beamed ceilings, and sun-filled windows loosely dressed with white linen curtains create a soothing environment, opposite.

Guests have the choice of a soaking tub set into a raised platform or a separate shower enclosure with two shower heads spewing bracing hot water, above.

Decor borrowed from
far-flung places can turn
the nondescript bathroom
into a chamber of exotic
charm. The pedestal
that designer John Saladino
chose to support a round
washbasin, left, appears
to be a fragment from
an archeological foray. The
washbowl on its marble
stand might be mistaken
for an ancient Roman font.
The votive shape of the
wall sconces and the simple
stone ledge for towels
also underscore the notion
that this is not a powder
room at all but the vestige
of a lost civilization
one has happened upon.

The Casbah perhaps
was Frédéric Méchiche's
inspiration for the decoration
of the beguiling bathroom
at his retreat in the south
of France, opposite. Brushed-
on Arabic-like designs
in scarlet hover on pistachio
rough plaster walls. Light
twinkles mysteriously
through the colored glass-
and-metal light fixtures, and
the Moroccan-style looking
glass seems to be a magical
portal to another world.

Like the inconstant sea, the tiles in Paola Navone's bath, opposite, shift from blue-gray to sapphire. The architect and design consultant transformed the bath of her Milan apartment into a haven by sheathing walls in small square tiles imported from Morocco. White grout and a slightly uneven application created an interesting, textured finish. The watery-blue tile sets off a collection of turquoise pottery crowding shelves above a deep tub the color of a cerulean ocean.

In his sixteenth-century Provençal farmhouse retreat, Paris couturier Michel Klein installed an array of blue-and-white decorative tiles as an enclosure for an old-fashioned tub, above right. The occasional squares of solid blue makes the mix more appealing. Even the stepping stone to the high tub is paved in broken crockery.

Large mosaic shards form a vividly colored abstract mosaic in a shower stall designed by Debra Yates for her own Key West home, below right.

The European eighteenth-century taste for rocaille and coquille—rockwork and shellwork—inspired the grottolike decoration of two small powder rooms pictured here. A scheme that designer Celeste Cooper sketched on wallboard took form with pebbles purchased at a garden center, opposite. A contractor cemented the pebble picture in place, grouted it, and secured it to the wall. A hammered nickel basin lining a cement pedestal is more fountain than sink, and perfect for a grotto fantasy.

Designers Jed Johnson and Alan Wanzenberg transformed a tiny room in a Southampton beach house into a unique space, above and left, using patterns of meticulously glued-on shells. The trellised dado, mirror frame, and pilasters framing the window—even the spiky chair rail—are part of the intricate seashell mosaic.

imp

"How do I get my bathroom to look like *that*?" Readers who have been inspired by the ideas presented in this book may well wonder how to proceed. Bathroom design can be as formidable as new construction, as challenging as a search for antique fixtures, as exciting as a cosmetic renovation, or as gratifying as luxurious new towels. Sweeping changes can be made all in one stage, or incrementally, over a period of time. The first step in every significant bathroom scheme is the same, though: a

lementing

consideration of all the options. For most of us, this requires the involvement of a professional, someone who can serve as a guide through the labyrinth of construction, equipment, zoning, and installation constraints. Because of its personal nature, the bathroom should be furnished with great care, and we have collected our favorite resources for fixtures and fittings, tiles and accessories, manufactured and custom appliances. Many are themselves the source of the bathroom fittings featured in the previous pages, and all will welcome your inquiries.

antique
tubs & sinks

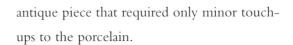

antiques aficionados who feel that the designs of old—claw-foot tubs, pedestal sinks, and the like—have never been surpassed can bring that appreciation to the bathroom. The trend in recent bathroom decoration has been to move away from utilitarian features and focus on the grand. This has brought an influx of old fixtures and salvaged pieces to the market; and inspired manufacturers to produce a wide range of reproduction models. The deep, oversize tub, opposite, is one example of an

antique piece that required only minor touch-ups to the porcelain.

Tubs came into wide use in the late 1800s, so it's possible to find one that is 100 years old. The condition of an old tub can vary greatly. If it has been well preserved, it may need nothing more than a fresh coat of paint on the outside. If the inside of the tub has a few minor cracks, it is better to fill them in than to refinish the whole tub, as refinishing is expensive and often must be repeated every few years since the bond between an old and new coat of porcelain is tenuous at best. If, however, the tub has serious cracks or rust stains (particularly around the drain), professional restoration is necessary.

Dirt can hide cracks and rust stains, so make sure a tub is clean before you purchase it. A few small cracks are okay—they may even add to a tub's character. But circular cracks are a bad sign; they indicate that the tub has been dropped and deep damage has occurred. Feel for the smoothness of a tub's surface—naturally, the smoother it feels against your hand, the better it will feel against your skin.

some considerations

When tub shopping, choose cast iron over steel; it is sturdier and retains heat better. A simple test: knock on the tub. A hollow sound indicates steel. A thud means it's cast iron.

Matching missing fittings, such as faucet handles or tub feet, is difficult but possible. Some antique dealers offer matching services: If you give them a picture of the item you want to match, they will find it for you. Locating missing claw feet, however, can take some time. It might be easier to start over with a set of four, either a different but appropriate antique set or an antique reproduction.

Repainting the outer surface of an antique tub should be done with an oil-based paint (preferably high gloss) for durability and water resistance.

Reglazing is something of a misnomer. Technically, glazing means firing, which if done to an original finish would actually crack it.

To restore an old finish, professionals begin by sanding down the surface and then covering it with a paint and epoxy compound that can vary greatly in quality, cost, and durability, depending on the restorer.

Moving tubs can be tricky. Hire a professional and have the tub insured. If it is dropped, tiny cracks will radiate up from the bottom. The damage may not be visible immediately, but over time the surface will crack and buckle.

Installation of antique fixtures should be handled only by certified plumbers.

Old tubs and sinks should be cleaned only with non-abrasive cleansers; bleach and products containing bleach should never be used on porcelain or marble surfaces.

site-specific installation

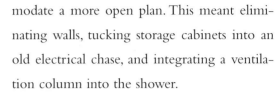

Sometimes a simple bathroom touch-up won't do. If your existing bathroom is not what you want it to be, or you are beginning a new construction project, a site-specific installation may be in order.

The bathroom here, for example, was created by designer Beata Galdi for a loft-dwelling client who wanted a big shower experience and more space. To get started, Galdi encourages clients to think about how they want to feel in the finished space. In this case, the client's response was "serene."

Confronted with a series of five separate rooms, which created a busy, cramped feeling, Galdi structurally altered the space to accom-modate a more open plan. This meant elimi-nating walls, tucking storage cabinets into an old electrical chase, and integrating a ventila-tion column into the shower.

To build the illusion of a larger space, Galdi installed a large, softly curving glass "cur-tain" to define the shower without cutting the room in half. Custom-cut slate floor tiles, sized proportionally to the room, were laid crosswise to visually expand the narrow corridor effect of the space. To create the "big shower experi-ence" her client requested, Galdi integrated three strategically placed massage-type shower heads. To keep the room serene and unfettered, she designed the surfaces to meet each other with as few visible seams as possible. And she installed a sliding opaque glass wall in the place of a traditional one to introduce light into the windowless space.

As Galdi notes, "Each installation has different requirements. We have to devise new systems for each job."

In addition to creating a unique look, site-specific design affords the opportunity to update old plumbing, wiring, and ventilation systems. Reordering the underlying elements can be as important to the style, comfort, and functionality of a bathroom as the custom sur-face details that make the room dazzle.

resources

AF Supply New York
22 West 21st Street
New York, NY 10010
(800) 366-2284
Fixtures, faucets, hardware,
accessories

Agape
220 Deerwood Street
Columbia, SC 29205
(803) 738-1818
www.agapedesign.it
Fixtures, furniture, mirrors,
lighting, accessories

Alsons Corporation
42 Union Street
Hillsdale, MI 49242
(800) 421-0001
www.alsons.com
Contemporary mirrors, hand-
held massage shower fixtures,
shower heads

Alternative Designs
2041 West Carroll Street
Chicago, IL 60612
(312) 733-9585
www.alternative-designs.com
Opaque, translucent, and
etched glass for vanities,
countertops, basins, and
shower enclosures

Amerec Sauna and Steam
P.O. Box 40569
Bellevue, WA 98015
(800) 331-0349
www.amerec.com
Custom and stock saunas, accessories, and steam generators

American Chinaware
6615 West Boston Street
Chandler, AZ 85226
(800) 359-3261
Custom, hand-painted, and
stock fixtures

American Standard
1 Centennial Avenue
Piscataway, NJ 08855
(800) 524-9797
www.americanstandard-us.com
Fixtures, faucets

Ann-Morris Antiques
239 East 60th Street
New York, NY 10022
(212) 755-3308
Custom lighting systems,
antique fixtures

Ann Sacks Tile & Stone
8120 Northeast 33rd Drive
Portland, OR 97211
(800) 278-TILE
www.annsackstile.com
Additional showrooms
Antique, handmade, stone, ceramic,
glass, metal, and terracotta tile

Aqua Glass
P.O. Box 412
Industrial Park
Adamsville, TN 38310
(901) 632-0911
Fiberglass and acrylic whirlpools
and shower doors, steam units

Aquaware America
1 Selleck Street
Norwalk, CT 06855
(800) 527-4498
Italian fixtures, mirrors, and
accessories

Architectural Salvage
1 Mill Street
Exeter, NH 03833
(888) 733-5635
www.oldhousesalvage.com
Restored and unrestored
fixtures, faucets, lighting, and
hardware

The Art of Glass
2331 Hartland Street
West Hills, CA 91307
(818) 551-4527
www.artofglass.com
Custom leaded, stained, beveled,
etched, and engraved glass

Ballard Designs
1670 DeFoor Avenue NW
Atlanta, GA 30318
(800) 367-2810
www. ballard-designs.com
Reproduction accessories

The Bath & Beyond
135 Mississippi Street
San Francisco, CA 94107
(415) 552-5001
www.bathandbeyond.com
Fixtures, faucets, accessories

Bathroom Machineries
495 Main Street
Murphys, CA 95247
(800) 255-4426
www.deabath.com
Antique and reproduction
fixtures, faucets, accessories,
lighting, and hardware

Baths from the Past
83 East Water Street
Rockland, MA 02370
(800) 697-3871
www.bathsfromthepast.com
Reproduction fixtures, faucets,
and accessories

Bis Bis/Isole
4 Park Plaza
Boston, MA 02116
(888) BIS-9909
www.bisbis.com
Fixtures, faucets, furniture,
accessories

Bisazza
8530 Northwest 30th Terrace
Miami, FL 33122
(305) 597-4099
www.infobisazzausa.com
Glass tile, mosaics

Boffi New York
150 East 58th Street
New York, NY 10155
(212) 421-1800
Contemporary fixtures, faucets,
and accessories

Buddy Rhodes Studio
2130 Oakdale Avenue
San Francisco, CA 94124
(877) 706-5303
www.buddyrhodes.com
Pre-cast and handmade colored
concrete tile and slabs

Ceramica
7039 East Main Street
Scottsdale, AZ 85251
(602) 990-7074
Custom and hand-painted
ceramic tile, glass and stoneware
tile and mosaics

Cooper Lighting
400 Busse Road
Elk Grove Village, IL 60007
(847) 956-8400
www.cooperlighting.com
Lighting

Country Floors
8735 Melrose Avenue
Los Angeles, CA 90069
(310) 657-0510
www.countryfloors.com
Additional showrooms
Ceramic, terracotta, and marble
tile and sinks

Crossville Ceramics
P.O. Box 1168
Industrial Park
Crossville, TN 38557
(615) 484-2110
Porcelain tile and mosaics

CyberBath Catalog Ltd.
1963 Union Boulevard
P.O. Box 5031
Bay Shore, NY 11706
(800) 666-8864
www.baths.com
On-line source for fixtures,
faucets, accessories

Czech & Speake
350 11th Street
Hoboken, NJ 07030
(800) 632-4165
British reproduction faucets and
accessories

Davis & Warshow
150 East 58th Street
New York, NY 10155
(212) 688-5990
www.daviswarshow.com
Fixtures, faucets, accessories

Decoratta Ornamental Terra Cotta
115 East Main Street
Silverdale, PA 18962
(215) 453-0820
Custom handmade tile

Deer Creek Pottery
305 Richardson Street
Grass Valley, CA 95945
(530) 272-3373
www.aimnet.com/~tcolson/pages
/deercreek/dcpage.htm
Handmade tile, custom mosaics
and murals

Delta
55 East 111th Street
Indianapolis, IN 46280
(800) 345-DELTA
www.deltafaucet.com
Faucets

Design Source
115 Bowery
New York, NY 10002
(212) 274-0022
American, European, and
Japanese fixtures, faucets,
accessories, hardware, mirrors,
and vanity tops

Design Time
6800 Westside Road
Redding, CA 96001
(800) 520-TILE
Custom and stock ceramic tile
and mosaics

Dornbracht
1750 Breckinridge Parkway
Duluth, GA 30096
(800) 774-1181
www.dornbracht.com
Faucets, accessories

Duravit
1750 Breckinridge Parkway
Duluth, GA 30096
(888) 387-2848
www.duravit.com
Fixtures, furniture, accessories

Eljer
14801 Quorum Drive
Dallas, TX 75240
(800) 0-ELJER-2
www.eljer.com
Fixtures, faucets

The Faucet Depot
6141-A Kester Avenue
Van Nuys, CA 91411
(888) FAUCET-9
www.faucetdepot.com
Contemporary and reproduction
faucets and accessories

Firebird
335 Snyder Avenue
Berkeley Heights, NJ 07922
(908) 464-4613
www.firebirdtiles.com
Custom hand-painted tile

Franklin Brass
P.O. Box 4887
Carson, CA 90749
(800) 421-3375
www.franklinbrass.com
Accessories, safety products

The French Reflection
8901 Beverly Boulevard
Los Angeles, CA 90048
(800) 421-4404
www.frenchreflection.com
European makeup and shaving
mirrors

Gerber Plumbing Fixtures
4600 West Touhy Avenue
Chicago, IL 60646
(847) 675-6570
www.gerberonline.com
Fixtures, brass faucets

Ginger/GUSA
460-N Greenway Industrial Drive
Fort Mill, SC 29715
(888) 469-6511
Grab bars, hotel towel shelves,
hardware, accessories

Glass by Design
at The Trade Mark Antique Center
2121 West Beltway 8
Houston, TX 77043
(281) 586-8246
www.glass-by-design.com
Custom beveled and stained glass
for windows

Gracious Home
1220 Third Avenue
New York, NY 10021
(800) 338-7809
www.gracioushome.com
Contemporary and reproduction
fixtures, faucets, accessories, and
hardware

Grohe America
241 Covington Drive
Bloomingdale, IL 60108
(630) 582-7711
www.groheamerica.com
Faucets

Hansgrohe
1465 Ventura Drive
Cummings, GA 30040
(800) 719-1000
www.hansgrohe.com
Faucets, accessories

Hastings Bath Collection
30 Commercial Street
Freeport, NY 11520
(877) 222-6813
www.hastingstilebath.com
Additional showrooms
Fixtures, faucets, mirrors,
accessories, tile

Hewi, Inc.
2851 Old Tree Drive
Lancaster, PA 17603
(717) 293-1313
Tub and shower seats, mirrors,
hardware

Iberia Tile
2975 NW 77th Avenue
Miami, FL 33122
(305) 591-3880
Stone and ceramic tile and
mosaics

International Bath & Tile
7177 Convoy Court
San Diego, CA 92111
(619) 268-3723
Fixtures, faucets, accessories, tile

Jacuzzi Whirlpool Bath
2121 N. California Boulevard
Walnut Creek, CA 94596
(800) 288-4002
www.jacuzzi.com
Whirlpool baths, fixtures

Kallista
2446 Verna Court
San Leandro, CA 94577
(888) 452-5547
www.kallistainc.com
Contemporary and traditional
fixtures and faucets

Kohler Co.
444 Highland Drive
Kohler, WI 53044
(800) 4-KOHLER
www.kohlerco.com
Fixtures, faucets, massage
whirlpools

Kroin, Inc.
180 Fawcett Street
Cambridge, MA 02138
(800) OK-KROIN
Faucets, wash basins

Lefroy Brooks
10 Leonard Street
New York, NY 10013
(212) 226-2242
British faucets and accessories

L'Esperance Tile Works
1118 Rock City Road
Rock City Falls, NY 12863
(518) 884-2814
Victorian original and
reproduction ceramic tile

Liz's Antique Hardware
453 South La Brea Avenue
Los Angeles, CA 90036
(323) 939-4403
www.LAHardware.com
Antique, reproduction, and
contemporary hardware, bath
accessories, and lighting

Malibu Ceramic Works
P.O. Box 1406
Topanga, CA 90290
(310) 455-2485
http://home.earthlink.net/~mcworks
Custom hand-glazed repro-
duction tile

McIntyre Tile Company
55 West Grant Street
P.O. Box 14
Healdsburg, CA 95448
(707) 433-8866
www.mcintyre-tile.com
Custom handmade porcelain and
stoneware tile and mosaics

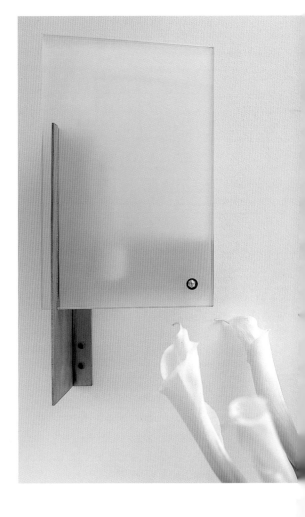

**Miotto 2000 Tile and Marble
Works**
926 26th Street
West Palm Beach, FL 33407
(561) 832-5511
Custom natural stone fabricators

Mission Tile West
853 Mission Street
South Pasadena, CA 91030
(626) 799-4595
Custom, hand-crafted, artisan,
and historical reproduction
tile and mosaics

Moen
25300 Al Moen Drive
North Olmsted, OH 44070
(800) BUY-MOEN
www.moen.com
Faucets, accessories

Nemo Tile Company
48 East 21st Street
New York, NY 10010
(212) 505-0009
www.nemotile.com
Additional showrooms
Porcelain, ceramic, glass, and
marble tile

New Ravenna
P.O. Box 1000
Exmore, VA 23350
(757) 442-3379
Marble, glass, and porcelain
tile and mosaics

Paris Ceramics
150 East 58th Street
New York, NY 10155
(212) 644-2782
www.parisceramics.com
Antique limestone and custom
hand-painted ceramic tile and
mosaics

Perrin & Rowe
1559 Sunland Lane
Costa Mesa, CA 92626
(800) 777-9762
www.rohlhome.com
Faucets, fixtures, accessories

Pewabic Pottery
10125 East Jefferson Avenue
Detroit, MI 48214
(313) 822-0954
Custom, handmade, embossed,
and field tile

Phylrich International
1000 North Orange Drive
Los Angeles, CA 90038
(800) PHYLRICH
Fixtures, accessories

Porcelain Industries
215 Union Boulevard
West Islip, NY 11795
(516) 661-4023
www.porcelainindustries.com
Antique and reproduction fixtures
and faucets

Porcher
6615 West Boston Street
Chandler, AZ 85226
(800) 359-3261
French-designed, custom hand-
painted fixtures

Portico Bed & Bath
139 Spring Street
New York, NY 10012
(888) 759-5616
www.porticonewyork.com
Additional showrooms
Bath linens, vanity cabinets,
accessories

Pottery Barn
P.O. Box 7044
San Francisco, CA 94120
(800) 922-5507
Additional showrooms
Accessories, hardware

Price Pfister
13500 Paxton Street
P.O. Box 4518
Pacoima, CA 91333
(800) 732-8238
www.pricepfister.com
Fixtures, faucets

Quality Refinishers
1930 Grove Court
Kissimmee, FL 34746
(407) 933-4146
www.clawtubs.com
Custom refinishing of antique
tubs and sinks, refinished antique
and reproduction fixtures

Resolute

1013 Stewart Street
Seattle, WA 98101
(206) 343-9323
Lighting

Restoration Hardware

15 Koch Road
Corte Madera, CA 94925
(800) 762-1005
www.restorationhardware.com
Additional showrooms
Accessories, hardware

Robern

7 Wood Avenue
Bristol, PA 19007
(215) 826-9633
www.robern.com
Mirrored bath cabinets, glass
consoles, lighting, accessories

Sherle Wagner International

60 East 57th Street
New York, NY 10022
(888) 9-WAGNER
www.sherlewagner.com
Fixtures, faucets, accessories, hardware, hand-crafted ceramic tile,
mirrors, lighting

Simons Hardware and Bath

421 Third Avenue
New York, NY 10016
(888) 2-SIMONS
www.simons-hardware.com
Contemporary and traditional
fixtures, faucets, tile, hardware,
lighting, and accessories

Soho Corporation

P.O. Box 1353
Water Mill, NY 11976
(800) 969-7646
British fixtures, faucets, and
accessories

Solar Antique Tiles

306 East 61st Street
New York, NY 10021
(212) 755-2403
www.solarantiquetiles.com
Antique and historical reproduction tile

Sonoma Tilemakers

7750 Bell Road
Windsor, CA 95492
(707) 837-8177
www.sonomatilemakers.com
Custom and stock ceramic tile

St. Thomas Creations

1022 West 24th Street
National City, CA 91950
(800) 536-2284
www.stthomascreations.com
Contemporary and traditional
china fixtures and faucets

Real Goods Trading Corp.

555 Leslie Street
Ukiah, CA 95482
(800) 762-7325
www.realgoods.com
Environmentally friendly
accessories, shower heads

Regent International

238 Beinoris Drive
Wood Dale, IL 60191
(800) 210-7054
Hand-held and wall-mounted
shower heads and massage units

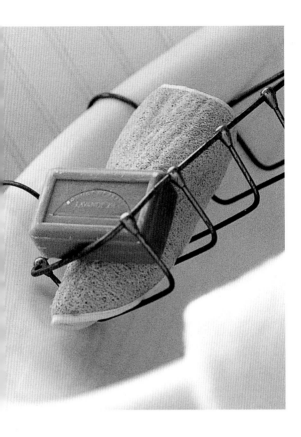

**Strom Plumbing
by Sign of the Crab**
3756 Omec Circle
Rancho Cordova, CA 95742
(800) 843-2722
www. signofthecrab.com
Solid brass reproduction faucets
and hardware

Sunrise Specialty
5540 Doyle Street
Emeryville, CA 94608
(800) 646-9117
www.sunrisespecialty.com
Reproduction fixtures,
faucets, and accessories

SWC Industries
1505 Industrial Drive
Henderson, TX 75652
(800) 999-1459
Acrylic tubs, whirlpools, and
shower bases

Tile Restoration Center
3511 Interlake North
Seattle, WA 98103
(206) 633-4866
Reproduction arts and crafts
tile, custom restoration

Toto USA
1155 Southern Road
Morrow, GA 30260
(800) 350-8686
www.totousa.com
Contemporary fixtures and
toilet seats

Urban Archaeology
143 Franklin Street
New York, NY 10013
(212) 431-4646
Antique and reproduction
fixtures, faucets, lighting,
mirrors, and accessories

Valley Bevelling Corporation
4626 South 33rd Place
Phoenix, AZ 85040
(800) 658-5839
www.crystal-city.com/vbchm-
frm.htm
Custom glass and mirror

Valli & Valli
1540 Highland Avenue
Duarte, CA 91009
(800) 423-7161
Mirrors, cabinets, lighting,
accessories

Walker & Zanger
8901 Bradley Avenue
Sun Valley, CA 91352
(800) 540-0235
Natural stone and ceramic tile

Watercolors
Garrison-on-Hudson, NY 10524
(914) 424-3327
Contemporary and traditional
fixtures, faucets, accessories,
mirrors, and lighting

Waterworks
29 Park Avenue
Danbury, CT 06810
(800) 899-6757
www.waterworks.net
Additional showrooms
Fixtures, faucets, tile, stone,
furniture, mirrors, lighting,
accessories

directory of designers

Leslie Armstrong
Armstrong Associates
New York, NY
(212) 353-4830

Gae Aulenti
Milan, Italy
(011 39) 25-280-2613

Howard Backen
Backen Gillam Architects
Sausalito, CA
(707) 967-1920

Matthew Baird
Tod Williams, Billie Tsien
    and Associates
New York, NY
(212) 528-3385

Barbara Barry, Inc.
Los Angeles, CA
(310) 276-9977

Barry Berkus
B3 Architects
Santa Barbara, CA
(805) 966-1547

Dana Berkus Interiors
Carbondale, CO
(970) 728-0924

Jeffrey Biben and Peggy Bosley
Biben + Bosley Architecture
Claremont, CA
(909) 624-8601

Lee Bierly, Christopher Drake
Bierly-Drake Associates
Boston, MA
(617) 247-0081

Bruce Bierman Design, Inc.
New York, NY
(212) 243-1935

Jeffrey Bilhuber
Bilhuber, Inc.
New York, NY
(212) 308-4888

Laura Bohn Design Associates
New York, NY
(212) 645-3636

Mark Bombara
Concord, MA
(978) 369-9553

Nancy Braithwaite Interiors
Atlanta, Georgia
(404) 355-1740

Turner Brooks Architects
New Haven, CT
(203) 772-3244

Mario Buatta, Inc.
New York, NY
(212) 988-6811

Stephen F. Byrns
Byrns, Kendall & Schieferdecker
    Architects
New York, NY
(212) 807-0127

Nina Campbell
London, England
(011 44) 1-71-225-1011

Victoria Casasco Studio
Venice, CA
(310) 399-1206

Walter Chatham Architect
New York, NY
(212) 925-2202

Fu Tung Cheng
Cheng Design and Construction
Berkeley, CA
(510) 849-3272

James C. Childress
Centerbrook Architects and
    Planners, LLC
Centerbrook, CT
(860) 767-0175

Jane Churchill Interiors Ltd.
London, England
(011 44) 1-71-730-8564

Celeste Cooper
Repertoire
Boston, MA and New York, NY
(617) 426-3865
(212) 826-5667

Carl D'Aquino Interiors
New York, NY
(212) 925-9787

Joan Dineen
Dineen Nealy Architects
New York, NY
(212) 396-2771

Mary Douglas Drysdale
Drysdale Design Associates
Washington, DC
(202) 588-0700

Joe D'Urso
D'Urso Design, Inc.
East Hampton, NY
(516) 329-3634

Melvin Dwork, Inc.
New York, NY
(212) 966-9600

David Anthony Easton, Inc.
New York, NY
(212) 334-3820

Paul Egee
Waterworks
Danbury, CT
(800) 899-6757

Steven Ehrlich Architects
Culver City, CA
(310) 838-9700

Richard Elmore Design, Inc.
Palo Alto, CA
(650) 321-8069

Maria Emmett Ltd.
New York, NY
(212) 288-0385

Heather Faulding
F2 Inc., Faulding Associates
New York, NY
(212) 253-1512

Ted Flato
Lake/Flato Architects, Inc.
San Antonio, TX
(210) 227-3335

John Funt
New York, NY
(212)371-6353

Beata Galdi Design, Inc.
New York, NY
(212) 254-9348

Arn Ginsburg
Santa Barbara, CA
(805) 964-1542

Mariette Himes Gomez
Gomez Associates
New York, NY
(212) 288-6856

Barry Goralnick
Goralnick/Buchanan Design LLC
New York, NY
(212) 644-0334

Gail Green
Green & Co., Inc.
New York, NY
(212) 909-0396

S. Russell Groves
New York, NY
(212) 966-6210

Eric Haesloop
Turnbull Griffin Haesloop
San Francisco, CA
(415) 986-3642

Joan Halperin Interior Design
New York, NY
(212) 288-8636

Mark Hampton, Inc.
New York, NY
(212) 753-4110

Barbara Hauben-Ross
Barbara Ross Interior Design
New York, NY
(212) 832-6440

Steven and Cathi House
House + House
San Francisco, CA
(415) 474-2112

Gerald N. Jacobs
Jacobs Design, Inc.
Tiburon, CA
(415) 435-0520

Hugh Newell Jacobsen
Washington, DC
(202) 337-5200

Jed Johnson and Associates, Inc.
New York, NY
(212) 489-7840

Ann Kalla
Cicognani Kalla Architects
New York, NY
(212) 308-4811

Brian Killian & Co.
Birmingham, MI
(248) 645-9801

Robert Kleinschmidt
Powell/Kleinschmidt
Chicago, IL
(312) 642-6450

Susan Lanier & Paul Lubowicki
Lubowicki/Lanier Architects
El Segundo, CA
(310) 322-0211

Evan LeDuc
Development Services
Benton Harbor, MI
(616) 849-3507

Mallory Marshall
Mallory James Interiors
Portland, Maine
(207) 773-0180

Ned Marshall Inc.
New York, NY
(212) 879-3672

Randolph Martz Architect
Charleston, SC
(843) 722-1339

Paul Mathieu
Aix en Provence, France
(011 33) 4-42-23-97-77

Frédéric Méchiche
Galerie Frédéric Méchiche
Paris, France
(011 33) 1-42-787-828

Catherine Memmi Boutique
Paris, France
(011 33) 1-44-07-22-28

Antonio Morello and
    Donato Savoie
Studio MORSA
New York, NY
(212) 226-4324

Elie Mouyal
Architecte DPLG
Amerchiche Marrakech, Morocco
(011 21) 2-430-0502

Brian Alfred Murphy
BAM Construction/Design, Inc.
Santa Monica, CA
(310) 459-0955

Paola Navone
Milan, Italy
(011 39) 25-810-4926

Mimmi O'Connell
Port of Call
London, England
(011 44) 1-71-589-4836

Marie-Paule Pellé
Paris, France
(011 33) 6-12-11-22-86

Thomas Pheasant, Inc.
Washington, DC
(202) 337-6596

Whitney Powers
Studio A, Inc.
Charleston, SC
(843) 577-9641

Julie Prisca
Paris, France
(011 33) 1-45-48-13-29

Rob Wellington Quigley
San Diego, CA
(619) 232-0888

Katie Ridder and Peter Pennoyer
New York, NY
(212) 779-9765

Jefferson B. Riley
Centerbrook Architects and
    Planners, LLC
Essex, CT
(860) 767-0175

Eve Robinson
New York, NY
(212) 595-0661

Ellen Roché Architect
Oyster Bay Cove, NY
(516) 922-2479

Van-Martin Rowe
Pasadena, CA
(626) 577-4736

John F. Saladino
Saladino Group, Inc.
New York, NY
(212) 752-2440

DeBare Saunders, Ronald Mayne
Stingray Hornsby Interiors
Watertown, CT
(860) 274-2293

Mark Sexton
Krueck & Sexton Architects
Chicago, IL
(312) 787-0056

April Sheldon Design
San Francisco, CA
(415) 541-7773

Elizabeth Speert, Inc.
Watertown, MA
(617) 926-3725

Michael Stanley
Putnam, CT
(860) 928-1419

Alexandra Stoddard, Inc.
New York, NY
(212) 289-5509

William Turnbull
Turnbull Griffin Haesloop
San Francisco, CA
(415) 986-3642

Ken Turner
London, England
(011 44) 1-71-355-3880

Alan Wanzenberg Architects
New York, NY
(212) 489-7840

Lester Wertheimer
Los Angeles, CA
(310) 208-4646

Samuel White
Buttrick White & Burtis
New York, NY
(212) 967-3333

Tod Williams, Billie Tsien and
    Associates
New York, NY
(212) 582-2385

Paul Vincent Wiseman
The Wiseman Group
San Francisco, CA
(415) 282-2880

Vicente Wolf & Associates
New York, NY
(212) 465-0590

Debra Yates
Key West, FL
(305) 296-5312

photography credits

1 Jon Jensen

2 William Waldron

4-5 Jeff McNamara

8 Tom McWilliam

10 Gary Quesada/
    Balthazar Korab Ltd.

12-13 Tim Street-Porter

14-19 Peter Margonelli

20 Kari Haavisto

21 Richard Felber

22-23 John Hall

24 Walter Smalling

25 Andrew Bordwin

26 John Vaughn

27 Langdon Clay

28-31 Tim Street-Porter

32-34 (left) Scott Frances

34 (right) Jacques Dirand

35 Peter Margonelli

36 Oberto Gili

37 Michael Dunne

38-39 Paul Whicheloe

40-41 Paul Warchol

42-45 Eric Roth

46-47 Christopher Irion

48 (left) Alexandre Bailhache
    (right) Oberto Gili

49 Robert Lautman

50 Oberto Gili

52-53 Tim Lee

54 Mark Samu

55-57 William Waldron

58-59 Jack Winston

60 (top) William Waldron
    (bottom) Peter Margonelli

61 Dominique Vorillon

62 Jesse Gerstein

63 (top) Scott Frances/Esto
    (bottom) Antoine Bootz

64-65 John Hall

66 Jeremy Samuelson

67 Peter Aaron

68 (top) Christopher
    Simon Sykes
    (bottom) Thibault Jeanson

69 Richard Felber

70 Oberto Gili

71-72 Christopher Irion

73 (top) Johnathan Hillyer
    (bottom) Peter Margonelli

74 Dominique Vorillon

75 John Sutton

76-77 Dominique Vorillon

78 Jeff Goldberg

79-80 Tim Street-Porter

81 Scott Frances

82-83 Peter Margonelli

84-85 Jesse Gerstein

86 Jeremy Samuelson

87 Antoine Bootz

88 Dominique Vorillon

89 John Vaughan

90-91 Jeff McNamara

92 Thibault Jeanson

93 John Hall

94 Tim Hursley

95 John Vaughn

96-97 Grey Crawford

98 Elyse Lewin

99 Laurie Dickson

100 Scott Frances

101 Courtesy of Toto

102 Jeff McNamara

103 Peter Margonelli

104 Scott Frances

105 Eric Roth

106 Lizzie Himmel

107 (left) Scott Frances
    (right) Jeremy Samuelson

108-109 Langdon Clay

110 Peter Wozynski

111 Domique Vorillon

112 Eric Roth

113 Oberto Gili

114 Scott Frances

115 (top) David Glomb
    (bottom) Dominique
    Vorillon

116-117 David Frazier

118 Jacques Dirand

120 Kari Haavisto

121 Jeff McNamara

122 Michael Mundy

123 (top) Michael Dunne
    (bottom) Jan Baldwin

124-125 Kit Latham

126-127 Dominique Vorillon

128-129 Marco Zecchin/
    Image Center

130 Tim Street-Porter

131 (top) Thibault Jeanson
    (bottom) Laura Resen

132 Antoine Bootz

133 William Waldron

134-139 Billy Cunningham

140 Tim Street-Porter

141 Scott Frances

142-143 Jacques Dirand

144-149 Fritz von der
    Schulenburg

150 Dominique Vorillon

151 Jacques Dirand

152-153 (top) Oberto Gili

153 (bottom) Richard Felber

154 Oberto Gili

155 Peter Margonelli

156 Fernando Bengoechea

158 Michael Mundy

159 John Vaughn

160-161 Peter Margonelli

162 (left) Thibault Jeanson
    (right) Walter Smalling

163 (left) Fernando
    Bengoechea
    (right) Courtesy of
    Delta Select

164 (left) Peter Margonelli
    (right) Courtesy of
    Kohler

165 Courtesy of Porcher

166 (left) Victoria Pearson
    (right) Dominique
    Vorillon

167 (left) Francis Amiand
    (right) Peter Margonelli

168 (left) Lizzie Himmel
    (right) Elizabeth Zeschin

169 (left) Elizabeth Zeschin
    (right) Scott Frances

171 Peter Margonelli

172 Jeff McNamara

175 James Merrell

176 Lizzie Himmel